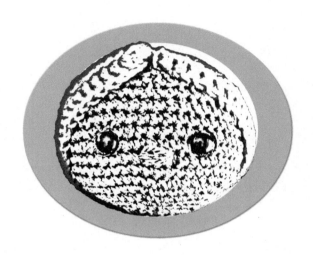

the **BIG** *Weebee Doll* book of hair patterns

A collection of hair caps and hair ideas for
the standard size Weebee doll

By Laura Tegg

Independently Published in 2023

Conceived, designed and produced by Laura Tegg

Copyright © Laura Tegg
ISBN: 9798870981147

*Dedicated to my lovely gran -
your life was a blessing, your memory is a treasure,
you're still loved beyond words & will forever be
missed beyond measure.*

Contents

Directory of hair patterns

Basic Hair
Pages 26 & 27

Elf Hair
Pages 30 & 31

Mermaid Hair
Pages 28 - 30

Angel Hair
Pages 32 - 34

Steam Punk Hair Cap
Pages 63 & 64

HRH The Queen
Pages 65 - 68

Most Versatile Hair Cap
Pages 69 - 74

Use the versatile cap to make the following 5 hair styles...

Straight Bob
Pages 75 - 77

Cornrow Braids
Pages 78 - 80

Twisted Hair Strands
Pages 81 & 82

Hair Wefts
Pages 83 & 84

Long Straight Hair
Pages 85 & 86

Ponytails, Pigtails, Plaits, Buns & Bunches

Ponytail
Pages 88 & 89

Hair Bun
Page 92

Pigtails
Page 89

Bunches
Page 93

Plaits & Braids
Pages 90 & 91

Space Buns
Page 94

Experimenting with Yarn
Pages 95 - 97

Introduction

My journey from hobbyist to crochet designer has not been an easy one. I tried several years ago to sell my crochet patterns and suffice to say it did not go well and I sold just a handful.

Eventually I gave up and made all of those early patterns available for free, resigning myself to a life of sitting in an office all day, every day doing a job that I didn't enjoy.

A few years later I designed a crocheted doll pattern for free, just for fun. I called the doll 'Weebee', after my niece Phoebe as when she was first born, my eldest niece and my daughter couldn't say her name properly and called her Weebee, so when looking for a non gender specific name for my doll, it seemed fitting.

People really liked Weebee and started asking for clothing for the doll. I designed a few patterns for free and they became so popular that I had to start charging for them as the admin on my Facebook page and designing patterns had suddenly become my full time job!

I have been so lucky and I would really like to take this opportunity to thank all of those who have supported me over the last seven years and in particular to my Facebook admin team and my testers who help me to ensure that my patterns are error free, understandable and user friendly.

I hope that the photo's and step-by-step instructions will help you to navigate your way through each stitch and I hope that you will see this book as a resource for extending your own skills and developing your own ideas.

Laura xx

Before you begin...

About this book...

This book begins with a chapter with information on the basic crocheting skills and stitches you will need to complete the patterns within this book as well as the special stitches and techniques used to create texture and interest.

This book compiles all of the hair patterns available for the standard size Weebee doll at the time of publishing. You can find the standard size Weebee doll pattern for free at ravelry.com or in the Hooked On Weebee book available from Amazon. The caps in this book will also fit several of my other dolls - please see page 24 for more information.

Equipment and materials

Crochet Hooks may be made from aluminium, steel, wood, bamboo or plastic. They are available in a variety of different sizes to suit different types of yarn and tension requirements. Sizes range from 0.6mm (the smallest), up to 15mm or more, and the hooks are normally between 125mm normally (5in.) and 200mm (8in.) long. The shaft behind the hook may be cylindrical, or with a flattened area to help you hold it at the correct angle. Try out different options to see what suits you best.

We don't have a vast choice here in the UK **yarn** wise, I tend to use acrylic yarns by Stylecraft Special and Paintbox for my dolls, they're lovely to work with, reasonably priced and have a good range of colours to choose from.

<u>Important Information</u>

I have tried very hard to make my patterns as versatile as possible. In theory as long as you use the same type of yarn e.g. acrylic, cotton etc., the same brand of yarn, the same weight of yarn and the same hook size, these hair patterns should fit your dolls. I also use acrylic yarn for my dolls and their clothing which has a lot of stretch to it. However If you tend to stuff your dolls very firmly, so that that the dolls body has very little give or use cotton yarn, it is highly recommended that you go up a hook size when making the patterns within this book.

Terminology: US

Other items needed
Stitch marker
Tapestry needle

Terminology

Although I am a designer based in the UK, I use US terminology within this book. On the next page you will find a handy conversion chart for those of you who are more familiar with UK terminology.

US Terms   UK Terms
Chain (ch)   Chain (ch)
Single Crochet (sc) Double Crochet (dc)
Half Double Crochet (hdc)   Half Treble Crochet (htr)
Double Crochet (dc)   Treble (tr)
Treble/Triple Crochet (tr)Double Treble (dtr)

Abbreviations

Chain (ch)
Double Crochet (dc)
Double Crochet Decrease (dc2tog)
Half Double Crochet (hdc)
Half Double Crochet Decrease (hdc2tog)
Loop (lp)
Magic ring (MR)
Next (nxt)
Round (rnd)
Single Crochet (sc)
Single Crochet Decrease (sc2tog)

Space (sp)
Stitch (st)
Slip Stitch (sl st)
Yarn Over (yo)

Yarn Weights & Hook Sizes

You can make your dolls bigger or smaller by using different yarn weights and hook sizes. On the page opposite you will find a chart that explains yarn weights and it gives a recommended hook size - **don't forget to size one or two hook sizes down for amigurumi to get nice tight stitches.**

Yarn Conversion Chart

USA	UK	Australia	Germany	Crochet hook size,
0 or Lace	1 ply			1.5 - 2.5
0 or Lace	2 ply		2 fädig (ply)	1.5 - 2.5
1 or Super Fine	3 ply	3 ply	3 fädig	2.25 - 3.5
1 or Super Fine	4 ply	4 ply	4 fädig	2.25 - 3.5
2 or Fine		5 ply	6 fädig	3.5 - 4.5
3 or Light	DK (Double Knit) or 8 ply	8 ply		4.5 - 5.5
4 or Medium	Worsted, Aran, Triple Knit (rare)	10 or 12 ply		5.5 - 6.5
5 or Bulky	Chunky, Double Double Knit (rare)	12 or 16 ply		6.5 - 9
6 or Super Bulky	Super Chunky			>9
7 or Jumbo				15 mm and larger

Hook Conversion Chart

Metric	US	UK
2.00 mm	B/1	14
2.25 mm		13
2.50 mm	C/2	12
3.00 mm		11
3.25 mm	D/3	10
3.50 mm	E/4	9
3.75 mm	F/5	
4.00 mm	G/6	8
4.25 mm		
4.50 mm	7	7
5.00 mm	H/8	6
5.50 mm	I/9	5
6.00 mm	J/10	4
6.5 mm	K/10.5	3
7.00 mm		2
8.00 mm	L/11	0
9.00 mm	M/13	00
10.00mm	N/13	000
12.00 mm	O/16	
15.00 mm	P/19	

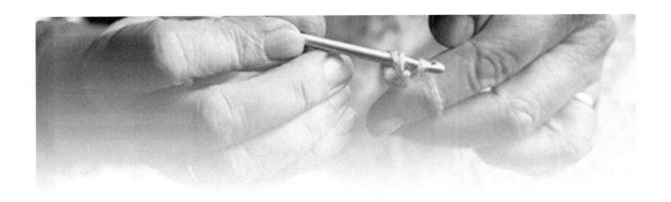

Special Stitches

Invisible single crochet decrease (sc2tog): Insert hook in front loop only of first st, insert hook in front loop only of second st (3 lps on hook), yo and draw through 2 lps, yo and complete sc as normal.

Sc3tog: *Insert hook into next st. yo hook and draw up a loop. repeat from * twice more into each of the next 2sts (4 lps on hook). Yo once more and draw through all 4 lps on hook.

3dc Bobble: Yo, insert hook into st and draw up a loop, yo and draw through two loops on the hook - two loops remain on the hook - *yo, insert hook into same st and draw up another loop, yo and pull through first two loops on the hook - three loops remain on hook*, repeat from * to * once more, you should have four loops on the hook, yo and pull through all loops on hook, yo again and pull through tightly to close the stitch.

Twisted Single Crochet (tw sc): Stitches are worked from the right to the left. Insert hook into st, yo, pull through a loop (2 loops on hook, make them loose), rotate the hook,, towards yourself and around 360 degrees, yo and draw through two loops on hook. For a video simply head to YouTube and search for 'Twisted Single Crochet'.

Front Post Double Crochet (fpdc): Yo, insert your crochet hook from front to back (right to left if you are a right-handed crocheter), so that it goes around the post that is positioned directly below it in the previous row of your crochet work, yo and pull through to finish.

To work 2fpdc simply a fpdc as above twice around the same st.

Front Post Half Double Crochet (fphdc): Yo, insert hook from front to back to front around post of corresponding stitch below, yo and pull up loop, yarn over and draw through all loops on hook.

Back Post Half Double Crochet (bphdc): Yo, insert hook from front to front to back around post of corresponding stitch below, yo and pull up loop, yarn over and draw through all loops on hook.

Herringbone Half Double Crochet (hbhdc): Yo, insert hook into stitch, yo, pull through (3 loops on hook), pull first loop through second loop on hook (without another yo), then yo and draw through 2 rem loops on hook.

Puff Stitch (PS): Yo, insert hook in st or space as indicated, YO and pull up a loop even with hook 4 times, yo and draw through all 9 loops on hook, ch1 to close.

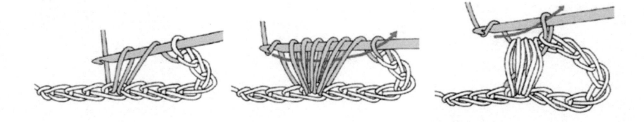

Special Techniques

Working into the Back Bumps of the Starting Chain

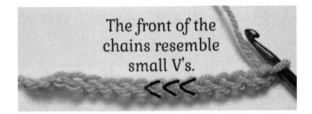

The front of the chains resemble small V's. <<<

In the first picture you can see the top of the chains, which resemble small V's. This is where you normally work your stitches into. But when working into the back bumps, you turn your chains over, as demonstrated in the next picture.

With the chains turned over, you see the back bumps sticking out on top. You'll insert your hook under these bumps when the pattern says to work into the back bumps.

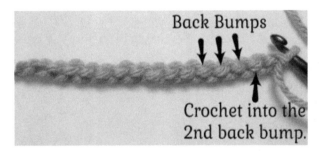

Back Bumps

Crochet into the 2nd back bump.

Back Bumps

Basically when you insert your hook you would have both the front loops (small V's) at the back of the hook and the back bump is on top of the hook.

Working into the Lower Back Loop

Like every other crochet stitch, the half double crochet has **two top loops**, the **front loop**, and the **back loop**.

These are the loops in which regular crochet normally happens.

However, **on the wrong side** of a half double crochet stitch, you'll find one extra loop compared to the other crochet stitches. This is the **third loop**.

For a video simply search YouTube for 'crochet third loop'.

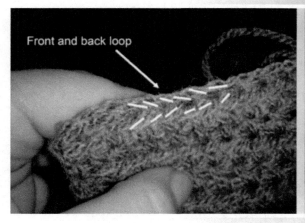

Front and back loop

Lower loop behind the back loop

Where can I find more Weebee Doll patterns?

You can find all of the Weebee doll patterns - over 40 of them for free including dolls and clothing items at

www.ravelry.com

Simply search for 'Weebee' or 'Laura Tegg'

~ • ~

You can find collections of Hair Caps for the Standard Size Weebee Doll as well as Birth & Adoption Certificates on

www.etsy.com and www.ko-fi.com

Simply search for 'Weebee Book of Hair' or 'Weebee Certificate'

~ • ~

Where can I find other Weebee fans?

If you're not already a member don't forget to join the **Weebee Appreciation Society group** on **Facebook**.

You can also join the **Hooked on Weebee Club** on **Patreon** for exclusive content, discounts and merch!

~ • ~

Where can I find useful videos for these dolls?

You can also find lots of helpful videos on the **Weebee & Friends YouTube Channel**

Frequently Asked Questions

Is the clothing removable? How does it go on over the dolls head?

All of the items in my doll clothing patterns are removable. The clothing items are designed to go on over their feet.

Will a pattern designed for one of your dolls fit one of your other dolls?

All of my dolls are different shapes and sizes so an item of clothing designed for one won't fit another without a great deal of adjustment. However, the hair caps within this book will fit several of the Weebee dolls - please see page 24.

How do I know which clothing pattern will fit which doll?

I always prefix the pattern name with the name of the doll e.g. Weebee Doll -, Little Weebee Doll - etc. I also say in every pattern description before you download or purchase which doll a pattern is designed to fit. I also start every pattern with a 'Before you Begin' heading where, I again explain which doll the pattern is designed for.

What type of yarn and hook size should I use?

You just need to use a combination of yarn and hook size that gives you nice tight stitches – every crocheter is different, what works for one person might not work for another. It took me a few attempts to find the perfect combination for my dolls and it may be the same for you. The size of your doll will be dependant upon the weight of yarn you choose, the brand of yarn you use (as they can differ vastly) as well as the hook size you choose and your own personal gauge/ tension. How firmly you stuff and shape your dolls plays an important part too of course. The tighter your stitches are the easier it will be

to stuff your doll firmly and **shape it as you stuff**. A firmly stuffed, well shaped doll will feel like an orange when pressed and will be much less likely to have a wobbly head.

I've started making a Weebee but but it looks really odd! The head looks huge! Is this normal?

Some of the Weebee dolls heads can appear particularly huge before you add the hair and clothing. So don't worry, trust in the pattern and I'm sure you'll be pleased with the end result.

I don't like the shape of my doll...the neck's too long, it doesn't have a tummy and bottom, what did I do wrong?

One of the things I always say is to stuff, stuff, stuff and stuff until you can stuff no more but one of the things I don't think a lot of people realise is that you need to shape your doll as you stuff. Shaping is as important as stuffing firmly. You can't just put the stuffing in there and expect it to conform to the shape of the doll, you have to give it a helping hand. When people contact me unhappy about the shape of their dolls I always guide them in the direction of the video tutorial on the **Weebee and Friends YouTube channel** where you can watch me stuff and shape my doll.

If there's anything you're unhappy about with regards to your dolls, invisible decreases, colour changes, stuffing, shaping, making the hair caps, etc. you'll find helpful videos on the above mentioned YouTube channel.

Where can I find a tutorial for crochet eyes?

Head to YouTube and search for 'hodgepodge crochet eyes' - simply use different weights of yarn for bigger or smaller eyes.

My doll won't stand, how can I make it stand?

None of the Weebee dolls are designed to stand alone - please see information on page 52 for the only method I would recommend to help your doll to stand.

Where can I find the 3D Glitter Eyes you use?

I purchase my 3D Glitter Eyes from **Cello Express** online.

Why have I not been accepted into the Facebook group?

Please ensure that you answer all of the questions and agree to the group rules otherwise your request to join will be declined.

I saw a Weebee doll made into a TV/movie character, where can I find the pattern?

If you ever see a Weebee doll made into a popular tv or movie character, please note that the maker has always used their creativity to make their doll look that way. I don't design character patterns, free or paid, because of the obvious legal ramifications. Usually the poster will say which doll they used and will often describe in the post or in the comments on their post how they made them look that way.

Safety First

There are certain things you must consider when making your dolls, particularly if it is for child under the age of 3 or you are putting it up for sale and do not know who the recipient will be.

Start by checking if any kind of safety testing is required for handmade toys where you live - for example EN71 is the primary toy safety standard that is mandated to protect the consumer market in the UK at present. To find out what you need to comply with, simply head to your internet search engine and type in 'International Toy Safety Requirements' followed by your location e.g. 'UK'. If you fail to adhere to any legal requirements, you may incur fines or face the consequences if a child is harmed because of the toy. There are many helpful sites and groups online that can help you with this.

Be aware that safety eyes are not suitable for children under 3. Consider embroidering the eyes instead or simply crochet 2 black circles and sew them on. You can place markers in the stitches indicated within the pattern if you want to do these after completing the head.

Do not add foreign objects that are not designed for toy making to your dolls.
For example, wooden dowels, cardboard, any type of metal, rice or beans. These will not wash well, cause damp and may attract vermin and bugs. If you need to weigh your doll down in some way, use plastic beads that have been designed for this purpose poured into a clean stocking then tie it up tightly. For flat feet, cut discs of plastic canvas and sandwich them between two feet bottoms before continuing with the legs. Always use actual toy stuffing - do not use the stuffing from old cushions or pillows - actual toy stuffing will be clean and has been produced to toy safety standards and is likely to be hypoallergenic.

Please pause for a moment to read these two pages!

The patterns in this book have all been designed to fit the standard size Weebee Doll.

However, given the size of their heads they will also fit the following dolls - make sure to follow the advice on the opposite page for all of the dolls!

All patterns can be found at www.ravelry.com

Sitting Standard Size Weebee Doll

Medium Size Weebee Doll
- see pages 2-4 of doll pattern

Weebee - Tall Annie Doll

Weebee - Mae Doll

IMPORTANT INFORMATION!

As you work, try the caps on your doll to check the fit!

If it is working up too large –
try it again, going down a hook size or two.

If it is working up too small –
try it again, going up a hook size or two.

Things can work up differently due to chosen yarn brand and weight - different brands can differ vastly, even different colours in the same brand can work up differently. Your chosen hook size and your own personal gauge/tension will also effect how an item works up. Your personal gauge/tension can even change from hour to hour e.g. if you make something wide awake versus when you're tired.

The difference a hook size can make can be amazing and makes these patterns very flexible!

Feel free to work more or less repeat rows or rounds too,
to make the caps longer or shorter i.e. these are rows and rounds that have the same amount of stitches that you work to simply increase the length of something.

ATTENTION ATTENTION ATTENTION ATTENTION ATTENTION

Basic Weebee Hair

This hair cap is worked from the top down in joined rounds. At the end of each round join the last st to the top of the first with a sl st.

Rnd 1: MR, ch2 (not a st from now on), work 11dc, join (as above) (11sts)

Rnd 2: Ch2, work 2dc in each st around, join (22sts)

Rnd 3: Ch2, dc in the first st, work 2dc in the next st, *dc in the next st, work 2dc in the next st, repeat from * around, join (33sts)

Rnd 4: Ch2, dc in each of the first 2sts, work 2dc in the next st, *dc in each of the next 2sts, work 2dc in the next st, repeat from * around, join (44sts)

Rnd 5: Ch2, dc in each of the first 3sts, work 2dc in the next st, *dc in each of the next 3sts, work 2dc in the next st, repeat from * around, join (55sts)

Rnds 6+: Ch2, dc in the **back loop only** of each stich around, join (55sts) ^^Repeat round 6 until cap sits on the head at an angle like in this photo (I had 11 rounds in total at this point).

^^ You should be able to tell after working two or three straight rounds of 55sts whether or not the cap will be too big or too small.

TOO BIG? TOO SMALL? SEE PAGE 25

Sl st around **LOOSELY** to neaten the edge.

Fasten off leaving a long tail to make the parting and sew the cap to the dolls head.

Too big? Either try reworking the cap in a smaller hook size or pull back your work to round 4 and repeat straight rounds of 44sts in the back loop only from there to reduce the cap by 10 stitches.

Too small? Either try reworking the cap in a bigger hook size or pull back your work to round 5 (55sts) and work an extra increase round to increase the cap by 10 stitches. So round 6 would be Ch2, dc in each of the first 4sts, work 2dc in the next st, *dc in each of the next 4sts, work 2dc in the next st, repeat from * around, join (66sts) Then you would just work your straight rounds of 66sts in the back loop only until the cap fits as above.

To make the parting...

Attach a darning needle to your finishing tail and weave in and out of 4 rounds up the join on your cap, pull tightly to gather, then wrap the yarn around the gather several times until you are happy with how it looks - please see the video on the Weebee and Friends YouTube channel demonstrating how this is done.

Do not fasten off the tail...

To sew the cap onto the head...
Continue to use the finishing tail to sew the hair cap to head using a whip st – please see the video on the Weebee and Friends YouTube channel if you need help with this.

Fasten off and hide loose ends.

TOO BIG? TOO SMALL? SEE PAGE 25

Mermaid Hair

This hair cap is worked from the top down in joined rounds. At the end of each round join the last st to the top of the first with a sl st.

Rnd 1: Using chosen hair colour, MR, ch2 (does not count as a st from now on) work 11 dc, join as above (11sts)

Rnd 2: Ch2, 2dc in first st, 2dc in each st around, join last st to first with a sl st (22sts)

Rnd 3: Ch2, dc in first st, *2dc in next st, dc in next st, repeat from * around ending with 2dc in last st, join as before (33sts)

Rnd 4: Ch2, dc in first st, dc in next st,*2dc in next st, dc in each of next 2sts*, repeat from * around ending with 2dc in last st, join (44sts)

Rnd 5: Ch2, dc in first st, dc in each of next 2 sts,* 2dc in next st, dc in each of next 3 sts, repeat from * around ending with 2dc in last st, join (55sts)

Rnds 6 – 10: Ch2, dc in each st around, join (55sts)

Sl st LOOSELY around to neaten the edge.. Then fasten off leaving a long tail to make the gather and sew cap to dolls head.

Pin Curls – Make 6

Rnd 1: MR, ch2 (does not count as a st from now on) work 10hdc, join last st to first with a sl st (10sts)

TOO BIG? TOO SMALL? SEE PAGE 25

Rnd 2: Ch2, 3hdc in each st around, join last st to first with a sl st (30sts)

Rnd 3: Ch2, 3hdc in each st around, join last st to first with a sl st (90sts)

Fasten off.

Attach pin curls to hair cap – cap will not be sewn onto head at this point. Place 3 pin curls next to one another at the front of the hair line, work your stitches through the first round of your curls in and out between the two rounds at the bottom of your hair cap, so that the curls overlap the edge slightly to form a fringe (bangs).

Attach one pin curl to the very top of the cap, working your stitches through the first round of your curls in and out of the first round of your hair cap.

Place the last two pin curls below the top curl and above the three on the bottom, to fill up the gap in between (so you essentially have a triangle of curls on the cap as shown).

Pony Tail

Row 1: Ch31, hdc in second ch from hook and in each st across, turn (30sts)

Row 2: Ch1 (not a st from now on), work 3hdc in each st across, turn (90sts)

Row 3: Ch1, work 3hdc in each st across (270sts)

Fasten off leaving a long tail, attach darning needle and pass the yarn tail through the other end of row 3 to make a big loop of hair, as shown in

TOO BIG? TOO SMALL? SEE PAGE 25

above pic, then using the same tail and darning needle, sew pony tail in centre beneath the top pin curl at the back of the cap.

To sew the cap onto the head...

Continue to use the finishing tail from the cap to sew it to head using a whip st – please see the video on the Weebee and Friends YouTube channel if you need help with this.

Fasten off and hide loose ends.

This hair cap is worked from the top down in joined rounds. At the end of each round join the last st to the top of the first with a sl st.

Rnd 1: Using chosen hair colour, MR, ch2 (does not count as a st from now on) work 11 dc, join as above (11sts)

Rnd 2: Ch2, 2dc in first st, 2dc in each st around, join as before (22sts)

Rnd 3: Ch2, dc in first st, *2dc in next st, dc in next st, repeat from * around ending with 2dc in last st, join (33sts)

Rnd 4: Ch2, dc in first st, dc in next st,*2dc in next st, dc in each of next 2 sts*, repeat from * around ending with 2dc in last st, join (44sts)

Rnd 5: Ch2, dc in first st, dc in each of next 2 sts,* 2dc in next st, dc in each of next 3 sts, repeat from * around ending with 2dc in last st, join (55sts)

TOO BIG? TOO SMALL? SEE PAGE 25

Rnds 6 – 10: Ch2, dc in each st around, join (55sts)

Rnd 11: *Ch9, work 2sc in second ch from hook and in each ch back towards the brim of the cap, sl st back into same st, sl st into next st, sl st into next st and repeat from * around, ending with a sl st in last st (27 curls)

Fasten off leaving a long tail and sew into position on head.

TIP! If you want to, you can simply ch more in rnd 11 at the back of the head for a female elf with longer hair!

To sew the cap onto the head...
Continue to use the finishing tail from the cap to sew it to head using a whip st – please see the video on the Weebee and Friends YouTube channel if you need help with this.

Fasten off and hide loose ends.

TOO BIG? TOO SMALL? SEE PAGE 25

Angel Hair

This angel hair cap is made by combining two differently sized caps at an angle on the head with a bun and curls added afterwards sewing the caps together and onto the head. Both caps are made in joined rounds, at the end of each round join the last st to the first with a sl st.

First Cap - smaller

Rnd 1: Using chosen hair colour, MR, ch1 (does not count as a st from now on) work 11hdc, join as above (11sts)

Rnd 2: Ch1, 2hdc in first st, 2hdc in each of the remaining sts around, join as before(22sts)

Rnd 3: Ch1, hdc in first st, *2hdc in next st, hdc in next st, repeat from * around ending with 2hdc in last st, join (33sts)

Rnd 4: Ch1, hdc in first st, hdc in next st,*2hdc in next st, hdc in each of next 2 sts*,

repeat from * around ending with 2hdc in last st, join (44sts)

Rnd 5: Ch1, hdc in first st, hdc in each of next 2 sts,* 2hdc in next st, hdc in each of next 3 sts, repeat from * around ending with 2hdc in last st, join (55sts)

TOO BIG? TOO SMALL? SEE PAGE 25

Rnds 6 – 11: Ch2, hdc in the **back loop only** of each st around, join (55sts)

Rnd 12: Ch1, work tw sc (see special stitches) in each st around, joining last st to first with a sl st (55sts)

Fasten off and hide loose ends.

Second Cap - larger

Repeat rounds 1 – 5 of first cap.

Rnds 6 -15: Ch2, hdc in the **back loop only** of each st around, join as before (55sts)

Rnd 16: Ch1, work tw sc in each st around, join (55sts)

Fasten off and hide loose ends.

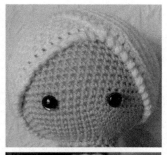

Position the two hair caps as you'd like them on the dolls head, both at an angle, like so. I placed the larger of the two beneath the smaller one.

When you are happy with the placement of the two caps take a length of the same coloured yarn and being careful not to catch the stitches on the head, sew the two caps together with a whip stitch, working through the stitches on the outer edge of the upper cap through stitches on the lower.

Then sew the cap to the head with a length of the same coloured yarn. There iis a video showing how I sewed this particular hair cap on, on the Weebee and Friends YouTube Channel.

T O O   B I G ?   T O O   S M A L L ?   S E E   P A G E   2 5

Curls – make two sets of four curls (8 curls in total)

*Ch15, work 2sc in second ch from hook and in each remaining st across, sl st into base of first stitch in chain (it doesn't really matter how neatly this is done as they'll all sit together and be sewn onto the head here anyway), repeat from * three more times before fastening off leaving a long tail for sewing (4 lots of curls)

The two lots of curls should be sewn onto the head next to one another in the gap where the two caps meet at the back, at the base of the neck, to one side.

Please see the video on the Weebee and Friends where I show how to sew on the curls, the video shows the actual doll in this pattern and where they need to be sewn on.

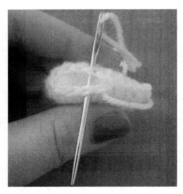

Bun

Rnd 1: MR work 6hdc, join last st to first with a sl st (6sts)

Rnd 2: Ch1 (not a st from now on), work 2hdc into each st around, joining last st to first with a sl st (12sts)

Rnd 3: Ch1, hdc into each st around, joining last st to first with a sl st (12sts)

Fasten off, leaving a long tail for sewing.

Lightly stuff the bun, and then sew 6sts either side together, forming the bun into an oval shape.

Sew the bun just above where the curls meet the hair cap.

Fasten off and hide loose ends.

TOO BIG? TOO SMALL? SEE PAGE 25

Beach Wear Hair

This hair cap is worked in joined rounds, at the end of each round join the last st to the first with a sl st.

Rnd 1: MR, ch2 (not a st from now on), work 14dc, join (as above) (14sts)

Rnd 2: Ch2, fpdc (see special stitches) in first st, ch1, *fpdc in next st, ch1, repeat from * around, join (14sts & 14ch1)

Rnd 3: Ch2, work 2 fpdc around first fpdc, dc in ch1, *work 2fpdc around next fpdc, dc in ch1, repeat from * around, join (42sts)

Rnd 4: Ch2, fpdc around each of first 2 sts, work 2 dc in next st, *fpdc around each of the next 2 sts, work 2dc in next st, repeat from * around, join (56sts)

Rnd 5: Ch2, fpdc around first st, 2fpdc around next st, dc in each of the next 2 sts, * fpdc around next st, 2fpdc around next st, dc in each of the next 2 sts, repeat from * around, join (70sts)

Rnds 6 & 7: Ch2, fpdc around each of the first 3 sts, dc in each of the next 2 sts, * fpdc around each of the next 3 sts, dc in each of the next 2 sts, repeat from * around, join (70sts)

TOO BIG? TOO SMALL? SEE PAGE 25

Rnd 8: Ch2, fpdc around each of the first 3 sts, dc2tog, *fpdc around each of the next 3 sts, dc2tog, repeat from * around, join (56sts)

Rnds 9 – 16 (or work as few or many rounds as looks necessary): Ch2, fpdc around each of the first 3 sts, dc in next st, *fpdc around each of the next 3 sts, dc in next st, repeat from * around, join (56sts)

Rnd 17: Ch1 (not a st), work tw sc (see special stitches) in each st around, join (56sts)

Fasten off, leaving a long tail to sew to make the parting and sew onto the head.

Use the tail to make a parting by gathering up the last four working rounds weaving in and out of the cap, then wrap the yarn around the gather – please see the video on the Weebee and Friends YouTube channel if you need help with this.

Then use the remainder of your tail to sew the cap onto the head using a whip stitch – please see the video on the Weebee and Friends YouTube channel if you need help with this.

Fasten off and hide loose ends.

Tendrils

Rnd 1: MR, work 6sc, join last st to first with a sl st (6sts)

TOO BIG? TOO SMALL? SEE PAGE 25

Rnd 2: *Ch31, work ^^2hdc in each of the first 15sts, hdc in each remaining ch back towards the circle, sl st back into same st and repeat from *once more into the same st before sl st into next st. Repeat from * in every st around, sl st into first st after working the last tendril (12 tendrils)

(^^if you find that working 2hdc is not curly enough, you can try working 3hdc instead. Alternatively you can go down a hook size or two to create tighter stitches)

Fasten off leaving a long tail.

Weave the tail in and out around the first round of stitches (6sts) and pull tight to gather it together, then insert your needle through the point created in the centre of the circle before sewing the tendrils onto the top of the hair cap, working through stitches on the cap and the head for a secure fastening - there is a video on the Weebee and Friends YouTube channel that shows how I sew my curls on.

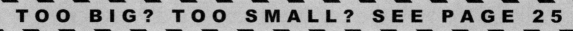

TOO BIG? TOO SMALL? SEE PAGE 25

Cupcake Hair

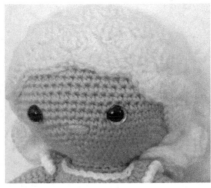

Worked from the top down in joined rounds, at the end of each round, join the last st to the first with a sl st.

Rnd 1: MR, ch2 (not a st from now on), work 12dc, join (as above) (12sts)

Rnd 2: Ch2, work 2dc in each st around, join (24sts)

Rnd 3: Ch2, dc in first st, 2dc in next st, *dc in next st, 2dc in next st, repeat from * around, join (36sts)

Rnd 4: Ch2, dc in each of the first 2sts, 2dc in next st, *dc in each of the next 2sts, 2dc in next st, repeat from * around, join (48sts)

Rnd 5: Ch2, dc in each of the first 3sts, 2dc in next st, *dc in each of the next 3sts, 2dc in next st, repeat from * around, join (60sts)

Rnd 6: Ch1 (not a st from now on), sc in first st, skip 2sts, work 5dc in next st, skip 2sts, *sc in next st, skip 2sts, work 5dc in next st, skip 2sts, repeat from * around, join (10 shells)

Rnd 7: Ch2, work 3dc in first st, *sc in top of 3rd dc of 5dc shell, work 5dc in next sc, repeat from * around, ending with 2dc in first st of round, join (10 shells)

Rnd 8: Ch1, sc in first st, *work 5dc in next sc, sc in 3rd dc of 5dc shell, repeat from * around, ending with a 5dc shell in final sc from last round, join (10 shells)

Keep trying the cap onto your doll's head as you can work as few or little rounds of shells until cap is desired length. Also If the cap is looking too big

TOO BIG? TOO SMALL? SEE PAGE 25

or small at any stage, you can try reworking it with a smaller or larger hook size as appropriate or work one less or one more dc increase rounds, as the shell stitch pattern repeat will still work with 48sts or with 72sts.

Rnd 9: Repeat round 7.

Rnd 10: Repeat round 8.

Rnd 11: Repeat round 7.

Fasten off leaving a long tail, then use the tail to sew the cap onto the head using a whip stitch – there is a video on the Weebee and Friends YouTube channel if you need help with this.

Fasten off and hide loose ends.

Curly Pigtail – make two

Pigtail is worked in joined rounds, at the end of each round join last st to first with a sl st.

TIP: For fuller curls you can work dc rather than hdc for these curly pigtails.

Rnd 1: Leaving a long starting tail, MR, ch1 (not a st from now on), work 6hdc, join (as above) (6sts)

Rnd 2: Ch1, work 4hdc in each st around, join (24sts)

Rnd 3: Ch1 (not a st), work 4hdc in each st around, join (96sts)

Fasten off and hide finishing tail.

Use starting tail to sew curl onto cap, above the shoulder – sew one onto each side working through stitches on both the cap and the head for a secure fastening – there is a video on the Weebee and Friends YouTube channel that shows how I sew my curls on.

TOO BIG? TOO SMALL? SEE PAGE 25

Halloweebee Hair

Hair cap is worked in joined rounds, at the end of each round, join the last st to the first with a sl st – please see the advice on the following page if the cap is looking too big or small as you start to work it.

Rnd 1: Using chosen yarn colour (I used white), MR, ch1 (not a st from now on) work 11hbhdc (see special stitches), join (as above) (11sts)

Rnd 2: Ch1, 2hbhdc in same st, work 2hbhdc in each remaining st around, join (22sts)

Rnd 3: Ch1, hbhdc in same st *2hbhdc in next st, hbhdc in next st, repeat from * around, ending with 2hbhdc in last st, join (33sts)

Rnd 4: Ch1, hbhdc in each of the first 2sts, *2hbhdc in next st, hbhdc in each of the next 2sts, repeat from * around, ending with 2hbhdc in last st, join (44sts)

Rnd 5: Ch1, hbhdc in each of the first 3sts, *2hbhdc in next st, hbhdc in each of the next 3sts, repeat from * around, ending with 2hbhdc in last st, join (55sts)

Rnd 6: Ch1, hbhdc in **back loop only** of each st around, join (55sts)

Rnds 7+: Repeat round 6 until the cap sits above the eyes at the front and

TOO BIG? TOO SMALL? SEE PAGE 25

above the neck at the back as pictured here.

Final Rnd: Ch1, work a tw sc (see special stiches) into each st around, join (55sts)

Fasten off leaving a good long tail to gather the parting and to sew cap to dolls head.

To make the parting gather up the last four rounds weaving in and out of the cap, then wrap the yarn around the gather – please see the video on the Weebee and Friends YouTube channel you need help with this.

Then use the remainder of your tail to sew the cap onto the head using a whip stitch – please see the video on the Weebee and Friends YouTube channel you need help with this.

Fasten off and hide loose ends.

Advice for hair caps...

My hair cap is too small!

If you find that the cap is too snug, you can pull back your work to round 5 (55sts) and work an extra increase round to increase the cap by 10 stitches. So round 6 would be Ch1, hbhdc in each of the first 4sts, *2hbhdc in the next st, hbhdc in each of the next 4sts, repeat from * around, ending with 2hbhdc in last st, join (66sts). Then you would just work your straight rounds until the cap fits as above. Alternatively you can remake the cap using a larger hook.

My hair cap is too big!

If you find that the cap is a bit roomy, you have two options, you can pull back your work to round 4 (44sts) and repeat the straight rounds from there

TOO BIG? TOO SMALL? SEE PAGE 25

to reduce the cap by 10 stitches. Alternatively you can remake the cap using a smaller hook.

Chain Loop Pigtails

These pigtails are crocheted in joined rounds, at the end of each round, join the last st to the first with a sl

Rnd 1: Using chosen colour for hair (I used white), MR, ch1 (does not count as a st from now on) work 10hdc, join last st to first with a sl st (as above) (10sts)

Curls: *Ch20 not too tightly, sl st into **front loop only** of next st – repeat from * all the way around, sl st into first st (10 curl loops)

Rnd 2: Ch1, work 2hdc into the **unworked back loop of each st in round 1** around, making sure to keep the curl loops at the front of the work as you do so, join last st to first with a sl st (20sts)

Curls: *Ch20 not too tightly, sl st into **front loop only** of next st – repeat from * all the way around, sl st into first st (20 curl loops)

Fasten off leaving a long tail for sewing the curly pigtails to the head.

Using a darning needle, sew the curls onto the cap working through the unworked back loops on the underside of the last round as pictured.

TOO BIG? TOO SMALL? SEE PAGE 25

Spring Festival Hair

Hair cap is worked in joined rounds, at the end of every round join the last st to the first with a sl st.

Rnd 1: MR, ch1 (not a st from now on), work 10hdc, join (10sts)

Rnd 2: Ch1, work 2hdc in each st around, join (20sts)

Rnd 3: Ch1, work a hdc in the first st, work 2hdc in the next st, *hdc in the next st, work 2hdc in the next st, repeat from * around, join (30sts)

Rnd 4: Ch1, work a hdc in each of the first 2sts, work 2hdc in the next st, *hdc in each of the next 2sts, work 2hdc in the next st, repeat from * around, join (40sts)

Rnd 5: Ch1, work a hdc in each of the first 3sts, work 2hdc in the next st, *hdc in each of the next 3sts, work 2hdc in the next st, repeat from * around, join (50sts)

Rnd 6: Ch1, work a hdc in each of the first 4sts, work 2hdc in the next st, *hdc in each of the next 4sts, work 2hdc in the next st, repeat from * around, join (60sts)

Rnd 7: Ch1, hdc in each st around, join (60sts)

^^**Rnds 8+:** Repeat round 7 until the cap sits on the head at an angle as pictured, I had 12 rounds in total before I started on the next round where we will make the tendrils (60sts)

TOO BIG? TOO SMALL? SEE PAGE 25

^^ Try the cap on your doll's head after working a couple of rounds of 60sts, if it looks too big at this stage, you may want to rework the cap using a smaller hook as appropriate and vice versa, if it looks too small, try reworking it using a bigger hook.

Last round: *Ch31, work ^^^2hdc in the second ch from the hook and then work 2hdc in each of the next 14chs, hdc in each remaining ch back towards the cap, sl st into the next st*, repeat from * to * until you have 20 tendrils, then ch1 and work a tw sc (see special stitches) in each of the next 20sts (this forms the front of the cap to give the impression of a fringe/bangs), sl st into the next st and repeat from * to * until you have 40 tendrils in total (40 tendrils and 20 tw sc)

^^^if you find that working 2hdc in each ch is not curly enough, you can try working 3hdc instead. Alternatively you can go down a hook size or two to create tighter stitches.

Fasten off, leaving a long tail to make the parting and sew the cap onto the head with.

Make the parting...
Attach a darning needle to a length of yarn the same colour as your cap and weave it in and out of the 4 rounds at the front in the centre, pull tightly to gather, then wrap the yarn around the gather several times until you are happy with how it looks – go online to watch a video on the Weebee and Friends YouTube channel demonstrating how this is done. Do not fasten off the tail...

Sew the cap onto the head...
Position the cap into the desired position and use the remaining fastening off tail to sew the cap onto the head, work your stitches through the last round of hdc's (before the last round of tendrils) and the stitches on the head for a secure fastening.

TOO BIG? TOO SMALL? SEE PAGE 25

Belle Hair

Hair cap is worked in joined rounds, at the end of each round, join the last st to the first with a sl st.

Rnd 1: Using chosen hair colour (I used brown), MR, ch1 (not a st from now on)
work 11hdc, join (as above) (11sts)

Rnd 2: Ch1, 2hdc in the **back loop only** of the first st, work 2hdc in the **back loop only** of each remaining st around, join (22sts)

Rnd 3: Ch1, hdc in the **back loop only** of the first st, work 2hdc in the **back loop only** of the next st, *hdc in the **back loop only** of the next st, work 2hdc in the **back loop only** of the next st, repeat from * around, join (33sts)

Rnd 4: Ch1, hdc in the **back loop only** of each of the first 2sts, 2hdc in the **back loop only** of the next st, *hdc in the **back loop only** of each of the next 2sts, 2hdc in the **back loop only** of the next st, repeat from * around, join (44sts)

Rnd 5: Ch1, hdc in the **back loop only** of each of the first 3sts, 2hdc in the **back loop only** of the next st, *hdc in the **back loop only** of each of the next 3sts, 2hdc in the **back loop only** of the next st, repeat from * around, join (55sts)

TOO BIG? TOO SMALL? SEE PAGE 25

Rnd 6: Ch1, hdc in the **back loop only** of each of the first 4sts, 2hdc in the **back loop only** of the next st, *hdc in the **back loop only** of each of the next 4sts, 2hdc in the **back loop only** of the next st, repeat from * around, join (66sts)

Rnd 7: Ch1, hdc in **back loop only** of each st around, join (66sts)

Rnd 8: Ch1, work (sc, dc, dc) in the first st, skip the next two sts, *work (sc, dc, dc) in next st, skip the next two sts, repeat from * around, join (66sts)

Rnd 9: Ch1, hdc in the **back loop only** of each st around, join (66sts)

Rnd 10: Repeat round 8 (66sts)

Rnd 11: Repeat round 9 (66sts)

Rnd 12: Repeat round 8 (66sts)

Rnd 13: Repeat round 9 (66sts)

Rnd 14: Repeat round 8 (66sts)

PLEASE NOTE: Feel free to work more or less repeats of rounds 8 and 9 as necessary dependant on the fit of the cap on your doll – it should look as pictured when placed on the head – yours may differ to mine in size due to yarn weight, hook size, personal gauge and how well the doll is stuffed.

Fasten off, leaving a long tail. Continue to use the finishing tail to sew the hair cap to the head using a whip st – please see the video on the Weebee and Friends YouTube channel if you need help with this. Secure and hide loose ends.

TOO BIG? TOO SMALL? SEE PAGE 25

Small Pin Curls – make 6

Rnd 1: With chosen colour for hair (I used brown), MR leaving a long starting tail, ch1 (does not count as a st from now on) work 8sc, join last st to first with a sl st (8sts)

Rnd 2: Ch1, work 3**hdc** in each st around, join last st to first with a sl st (24sts)

Rnd 3: Ch1, 3**sc** in each st around, join last st to first with a sl st (72sts)

^^If your curls are not curling enough, you have two options, you can work 4sts in each st around rather than 3 or you can try making them using a smaller hook as tighter stitches will mean a tighter curl.

Fasten off and hide your finishing tail.

Then using the long starting tail sew three curls on either side of your doll's

head at the front of the cap, slightly over-lapped, with a gap in the middle as pictured. Work your stitches through both the stitches on the cap and the doll's head beneath the cap for a secure fastening. Secure and hide loose ends.

Big Wide Curl

Rnd 1: With chosen colour for hair (I used brown), ch19, work sc in second ch from hook, sc in each of the next 16sts, work 3sc in the last st, turn to work down the opposite side of the

TOO BIG? TOO SMALL? SEE PAGE 25

chain, sc in each of the next 16sts, work 2sc in the last st, join last st to first with a sl st (38sts)

Rnd 2: Ch1, work 3hdc in each st around, join last st to first with a sl st (114sts)

Rnd 3: Ch1, work 3dc in each st around, join last st to first with a sl st (342sts)

^^If your curls are not curling enough, you have two options, you can work 4 multiples in each st around rather than 3 or you can try making them using a smaller hook as tighter stitches will mean a tighter curl.

Fasten off leaving a long finishing tail. Using the tail sew to the back of the doll's head as pictured.

Work your stitches through both the stitches on the cap and the doll's head beneath the cap for a secure fastening.

Secure and hide loose ends.

TOO BIG? TOO SMALL? SEE PAGE 25

Beau Hair

Hair cap is worked in joined rounds, at the end of each round, join the last st to the first with a sl st.

Rnd 1: Using chosen yarn colour (I used black), MR, ch1 (not a st from now on) work 11 hdc, join (as above) (11sts)

Rnd 2: Ch1, 2hdc in same st, work 2hdc in each st around, join (22sts)

Rnd 3: Ch1, hdc in same st *2hdc in next st, hdc in next st, repeat from * around, ending with 2hdc in last st, join (33sts)

Rnd 4: Ch1, hdc in each of the first 2sts, *2hdc in next st, hdc in each of the next 2sts, repeat from * around, ending with 2hdc in last st, join (44sts)

Rnd 5: Ch1, hdc in each of the first 3sts, *2hdc in next st, hdc in each of the next 3sts, repeat from * around, ending with 2hdc in last st, join (55sts)

Rnd 6: Ch1, hdc in each of the first 4sts, *2hdc in next st, hdc in each of the next 4sts, repeat from * around, ending with 2hdc in last st, join (66sts)

Rnds 7-14: Ch1, hdc in **back loop only** of each st around, join (66sts)

Rnd 15: Ch2 (not a st from now on), work 2dc in each of the first 2sts, work a hdc in each of the next 2sts, sc in each of the next 58sts, hdc in each of the next 2sts, work 2dc in each of the last 2sts, join (70sts)

Rnd 16: Ch2, work 2dc in each of the first 2sts, dc in each of the next 2sts, hdc in each of the next 2sts, sc in each of the next 58sts, hdc in each of the

TOO BIG? TOO SMALL? SEE PAGE 25

next 2sts, dc in each of the next 2sts, work 2dc in each of the last 2sts, join (74sts)

Rnd 17: Ch2, work 2dc in the first st, dc in each of the next 5sts, hdc in each of the next 2sts, sc in each of the next 58sts, hdc in each of the next 2sts, dc in each of the next 5sts, work 2dc in the last st, join (76sts)

Fasten off leaving a long tail to shape the front of the cap as follows and to sew it onto dolls head.

Don't panic as at first the cap will look very strange...

On the right hand side of the doll's head the downward curve at the front should be flat against the doll's face, then the other half of the curve should be curled upwards onto the cap as pictured.

When sewing the upward curve at the front sew beneath the edge so that it doesn't disappear into the stitches on the cap and looks instead like an overlap.

Continue to use the finishing tail to sew the hair cap to head using a whip st – please see the video on the Weebee and Friends YouTube channel if you need help with this.

Secure and hide loose ends.

TOO BIG? TOO SMALL? SEE PAGE 25

Sugar Skull Hair

Hair cap is worked in joined rounds from the top down, at the end of each round, join the last st to the first with a sl st.

Rnd 1: Using black yarn, MR, ch1 (not a st from now on), work 8hdc, join (as above) (8sts)

Rnd 2: Ch1, work 2hdc into each st around, join (16sts)

Rnd 3: Ch1, hdc into the first st, work 2hdc into the next st, *hdc into the next st, work 2hdc into the next st, repeat from * around, join (24sts)

Rnd 4: Ch1, hdc into each of the first 2sts, work 2hdc into the next st, *hdc into each of the next 2sts, work 2hdc into the next st, repeat from * around, join (32sts)

Rnd 5: Ch1, hdc into each of the first 3sts, work 2hdc into the next st, *hdc into each of the next 3sts, work 2hdc into the next st, repeat from * around, join (40sts)

Rnd 6: Ch1, hdc into each of the first 4sts, work 2hdc into the next st, *hdc into each of the next 4sts, work 2hdc into the next st, repeat from * around, join (48sts)

Rnd 7: Ch1, hdc into each of the first 5sts, work 2hdc into the next st, *hdc

TOO BIG? TOO SMALL? SEE PAGE 25

into each of the next 5sts, work 2hdc into the next st, repeat from * around, join (56sts)

Rnd 8: Ch1, hdc into each of the first 6sts, work 2hdc into the next st, *hdc into each of the next 6sts, work 2hdc into the next st, repeat from * around, join (64sts)

Rnd 9 – 13 (feel free to work more or less rounds as necessary)^^: Ch1, hdc into the **back loop only** of each st around, join (64sts)

^^ **Check the fit after working a couple of rounds, if it looks as if the cap will be too big or too tight, rework the cap using a smaller or large hook as appropriate.**

Rnd 14: Ch1, hdc into the **back loop only** of each of the first 15sts, work 3hdc into each of the next 34sts, hdc into the **back loop only** of each of the remaining 15sts, join (132sts)

Rnd 15: Ch1, **sc** into the **back loop only** of each of the first 15sts, work 3**dc** into each of the next 102sts, **sc** into **back loop only** of each of the remaining 15sts, join (336sts)

Rnd 16: Ch1, work a tw sc (see special stitches) into each st around, join (336sts)

Fasten off leaving a long tail to make the parting and sew the cap onto the head.

To make the parting…

Attach a darning needle to your finishing tail and weave in and out of 4 rounds up the join on your cap, pull tightly to gather, then wrap the yarn around the gather several times until you are happy with how it looks – see

TOO BIG? TOO SMALL? SEE PAGE 25

the video on the Weebee and Friends YouTube channel demonstrating how this is done. Do not fasten off the tail...

To sew the cap onto the head...

Use the finishing tail to sew the hair cap to head using a whip st – please the video on the Weebee and Friends YouTube channel if you need help with this.

Fasten off and hide loose ends.

Clown Hair

Made all in one go from the top to the bottom in joined rounds. At the end of each round, join the last st to the first with a sl st.

Rnd 1: MR, ch2 (not a st from now on), work 14dc, join as above (14sts)

Rnd 2: Ch2, work 2dc into each st around, join (28sts)

Curl Rnd: Ch17, skip the second st, sl st into the **front loop** of the next st, *ch17, skip the next st, sl st into the **front loop** of the next st, repeat from * around, join last ch17 to first st with a sl st as before (fourteen ch17 loops)

Rnd 3: Work entire round into back loops of round 2, holding the loops you made in the curl round to the front of the work. Ch2, work 2dc into each **back loop** around, join (56sts)

TOO BIG? TOO SMALL? SEE PAGE 25

~ 53 ~

Curl Rnd: Ch17, skip the second st, sl st into the **front loop** of the next st, *ch17, skip the next st, sl st into the **front loop** of the next st, repeat from * around, join last ch17 to first st with a sl st as before (twenty eight ch17 loops)

Rnd 4: Work entire round into back loops of round 3, holding the loops you made in the curl round to the front of the work. Ch2, dc in each of the first 6sts, work 2dc into the next st, *dc in each of the next 6sts, work 2dc into the next st, join (64sts)

Curl Rnd: Ch17, skip the second st, sl st into the **front loop** of the next st, *ch17, skip the next st, sl st into the **front loop** of the next st, repeat from * around, join last ch17 to first st with a sl st as before (thirty two ch17 loops)

Rnd 5: Work entire round into back loops of previous round, holding the loops you made in the curl round to the front of the work. Ch2, dc in each st around, join (64sts)

Curl Rnd: Ch17, skip the second st, sl st into the **front loop** of the next st, *ch17, skip the next st, sl st into the **front loop** of the next st, repeat from * around, join last ch17 to first st with a sl st as before (thirty two ch17 loops)

Rnds 6+: Repeat directions for round 5 and the curl round that follows until cap fits on your doll's head as pictured.

Final Rnd: Ch1, sc into the back loop only of each st (before the last curl round) around before fastening off and leaving a long tail to sew the cap onto the doll's head (64sts)

TOO BIG? TOO SMALL? SEE PAGE 25

Swirly Girl Hair

Hair cap is worked from the top down in joined rounds, at the end of each round join the last st to the top of the first with a sl st.

Rnd 1: MR, ch2 (not a st from now on), work 12dc, join as above (12sts)

Rnd 2: Ch2, fpdc around the first dc in the previous round, dc in the first space between the fpdc you just made and the next dc in the previous round, *fpdc around the next dc in the previous round, dc in the space between the fpdc you just made and the next dc in the previous round, repeat from * around, join (24sts)

Rnd 3: Ch2, fpdc around the first fpdc in the previous round, work 2dc into the first space
between the fpdc you just made and the first dc of the previous round, *fpdc around the next fpdc in the previous round, work 2dc into the next space between the fpdc you just made and the next dc of the previous round, repeat from * around, join (36sts)

Rnd 4: Ch2, fpdc around the first fpdc in the previous round, work 3dc into the first space
between the fpdc you just made and the first dc of the previous round, *fpdc around the next fpdc in the previous round, work 3dc into the next space between the fpdc you just made and the next dc of the previous round, repeat from * around, join (48sts)

TOO BIG? TOO SMALL? SEE PAGE 25

Rnd 5: Ch2, fpdc around the first fpdc in the previous round, work 4dc into the first space between the fpdc you just made and the first dc of the previous round, *fpdc around the next fpdc in the previous round, work 4dc into the next space between the fpdc you just made and the next dc of the previous round, repeat from * around, join (60sts)

Feel free to stop here and skip to the next round if you think the cap will fit at this stage without further increases or if it's too small after working round 6 please feel to increase further if you need to.

Rnd 6: Ch2, fpdc around the first fpdc in the previous round, work 5dc into the first space between the fpdc you just made and the first dc of the previous round, *fpdc around the next fpdc in the previous round, work 5dc into the next space between the fpdc you just made and the next dc of the previous round, repeat from * around, join (72sts)

Rnds 7+: Repeat the pattern directions for the last round worked until the cap fits on the dolls head as pictured.

Fasten off leaving a long tail.

Use the tail to sew the cap onto your doll's head.

To sew the cap onto the head...

Continue to use the finishing tail to sew the hair cap to head using a whip st – please see the video on the Weebee and Friends YouTube channel if you need help with this.

TOO BIG? TOO SMALL? SEE PAGE 25

Buttercup Hair

Worked in joined rounds from the top down, at the end of each round join the last st to the first with a sl st.

Rnd 1: MR, ch2 (not a st from now on), work 8dc, join (as above) (8sts)

Rnd 2: Ch2, work 2dc into each st around, join (16sts)

Rnd 3: Ch2, work 3dc into the first st, fpdc (see special stitches) around the next st, *work 3dc into the next st, fpdc around the next st, repeat from * around, join (32sts)

Rnd 4: Ch2, work 3dc into the first st, fpdc around the next st, work 3dc into the next st, fpdc around the next fpdc, *work 3dc into the next st, fpdc around the next st, work 3dc into the next st, fpdc around the next fpdc, repeat from * around, join (64sts)

Rnds 5 – 11^^: Sl st into the second st, ch2, work 3dc into the same st, skip the next st, fpdc around the next fpdc, skip the next st, *work 3dc into the next st, skip the next st, fpdc around the next fpdc skip the next st, repeat from * around, join (64sts)

^^ Feel free to work more or less rounds as necessary for your doll.

Last Rnd: Sl st into the second st, ch2, work 4dc into the same st, skip the next st, sc into the next st, skip the

TOO BIG? TOO SMALL? SEE PAGE 25

next st, *work 8dc into the next st, skip the next st, sc into the next st, skip the next st, repeat from * around, end with 4dc into the first st and join (144sts)

Fasten off, leaving a long tail. Sew the cap onto the head above the last round leaving the scallops in the last round loose.

Pigtail – make 2

*Ch42, work 3dc into the second ch from the hook, work 3dc into each remaining ch to end, repeat from * twice more to make 3 curls (120sts per curl)

Fasten off leaving a long tail to sew the pigtail onto the head. Use a darning needle and the tail, sew each pigtail onto each side of the head, a little more towards the front of the head onto round 4 of the hair cap – work your yarn through both the stitches on the cap and the stitches on the head for a more secure fastening. Secure tail and hide loose ends.

Tips

If your curls are not as tight as those pictured above, try reworking them in a smaller hook size and/or work 4dc per ch rather than 3dc.

If you find that your curls look odd when you're working them (see photos), you may have to twist the work in the right direction to pull them back into shape.

For a ponytail rather than pigtails, simply repeat from * until you have as many curls as you need and sew it onto the top of the head towards the back in the same way.

TOO BIG? TOO SMALL? SEE PAGE 25

Harry's Hair

This hair cap is worked from the top down in joined rounds, at the end of each round join the last stitch to the first stitch with a slip stitch.

Rnd 1: MR, ch2 (not a st from now on) work 15dc, join (as above) (15sts)

Rnd 2: Ch2, work 2fpdc (see special stitches) around each st in the last round, join (30sts)

Rnd 3: Ch2, fpdc around the first st, work 2fpdc around the next st, *fpdc around the next st, work 2fpdc around the next st, repeat from * around, join (45sts)

Rnd 4: Ch2, fpdc around each of the first 2sts, work 2fpdc around the next st, *fpdc around each of the next 2sts, work 2fpdc around the next st, repeat from * around, join (60sts)

Rnd 5: Ch2, fpdc around each st around, join (60sts)

Rnds 6+: Repeat round 5 until the cap fits on the head as pictured (60sts)

The cap is thick but stretchy so don't worry if it looks like it won't fit – see photos) but if you do find that it is too small and won't stretch, you will need to rework the cap with a larger hook, or if it's too big rework with a smaller hook.

TOO BIG? TOO SMALL? SEE PAGE 25

Last Rnd: Work your slip stitches **LOOSELY** – use a larger hook if necessary.

*Ch5, sl st into the second ch from the hook, sl st into each of the three remaining chs back to the hat, sl st back into the same st, sl st into the next st. Repeat from * 19 more times.

**Ch7, sl st into the second ch from the hook, sl st into each of the five remaining chs back to the hat, sl st back into the same st, sl st into the next st. Repeat from ** 4 more times.

***Ch9, sl st into the second ch from the hook, sl st into each of the seven remaining chs back to the hat, sl st back into the same st, sl st into the next st. Repeat from *** 4 more times.

****Ch11, sl st into the second ch from the hook, sl st into each of the nine remaining chs back to the hat, sl st back into the same st, sl st into the next st. Repeat from * 19 more times.

***Ch9, sl st into the second ch from the hook, sl st into each of the seven remaining chs back to the hat, sl st back into the same st, sl st into the next st. Repeat from *** 4 more times.

**Ch7, sl st into the second ch from the hook, sl st into each of the five remaining chs back to the hat, sl st back into the same st, sl st into the next st. Repeat from ** 4 more times.

You should have 60 strands of 'hair'.

Fasten off, leaving a long tail. With the tail at the centre at the back of the head, sew the cap onto the head above the last round of strands.

TOO BIG? TOO SMALL? SEE PAGE 25

Messy Bun Hair

This hair cap is worked in joined rounds from the top down, at the end of each round join the last st to the first with a sl st.

We will start by making a ring, we will work the bun onto the top afterwards.

Rnd 1: Ch24, join the last ch to the first with a sl st being careful not to twist the chain. Ch1 (not a st from now on), sc into each ch around, join as above (24sts)

Rnd 2: Ch2 (not a st from now on), work 2dc into each st around, join as before (48sts)

Rnd 3: Ch2, dc into each of the first 3sts, work 2fpdc around the next st, *dc into each of the next 3sts, work 2fpdc around the next st, repeat from * around, join (60sts)

Rnd 4: Ch2, dc into the first st, work a fpdc around the next st, dc into the next st, work a fpdc around each of the next 2sts, *dc into the next st, work a fpdc around the next st, dc into the next st, work a fpdc around each of the next 2sts, repeat from * around, join (60sts)

Rnd 5+: Repeat round 4 until the cap fits on the head as pictured .

TOO BIG? TOO SMALL? SEE PAGE 25

Do not be concerned if initially the cap tries to curl upwards in the wrong direction. Eventually it will even out the more rounds that you work.

Fasten off leaving a long tail for sewing to the head.

Messy Bun

The bun is made by crocheting long strands and then tying them together (all will be made clearer later).

Each strand is worked separately onto each of the stitches on the opposite side of the starting chain on the hair cap.

So with the cap held the right way round, attach your yarn to one of the stitches around the hole at the top of the cap.

*Ch41, sl st LOOSELY into the second ch from the hook, sl st into each remaining ch back to the hair cap, sl st into the next st, repeat from * around until you have 24 strands of 'hair'. To finish, sl st into the first st and fasten off. Hide the loose ends from the strands.

Sewing on the hair cap

Position the cap as desired at an angle on the head and using a darning needle attached to the fastening off tail sew the cap onto the head through the stitches around the edge of the cap and stitches on the dolls head.

Before securing and hiding the fastening off tail, pass it up to where the hole for the bun is and sew down the edge onto the doll's head **for a good secure fastening, this will also help when you tie the strands into a bun.**

TOO BIG? TOO SMALL? SEE PAGE 25

Steampunk Hair

This hair cap is worked from side to side initially then the first row and the last row are joined when it fits comfortably around your doll's head. The rows are then gathered together at the top.

Step 1: Leaving a long starting tail, ch35, work 2hdc into the second ch from the hook, work 2hdc into each of the next 3chs, hdc into each of the next 8chs, sc into each of the next 21chs, sl st into the last ch, turn (38sts inc last sl st)

Step 2: Ch1 (not a st from now on), sl st in the first sl st, sc into the **back loops only** of each of the next 21sts, ch13, turn and work 2hdc into the second ch from the hook, work 2hdc into each of the next 3chs, hdc into each of the next 8chs, sc into the **back loops only** of each of the next 21sts, sl st into the last st, turn (21sts, ch13, 38sts inc last sl st)

Following Rows: Repeat step 2 until the 'hair' fits around the dolls head as pictured above – check that you are happy with the coverage at the back and sides.

TOO BIG? TOO SMALL? SEE PAGE 25

Fringe/Bangs

Step 3: Ch1, sl st into the first sl st, sc into the **back loops only** of the next 14sts, sl st into the next st, turn (2 sl sts, 14sts)

Repeat step 3 until the 'hair cap' fits all the way around the doll's head as pictured.

Make sure to finish on a row that is at the bottom of the bangs as pictured.

Then take the two ends of your cap and bring them together, insert hook into the 16th st on the edge that is not on your hook and pull through a loop. Continue to sl st into each st along up to the top of the cap working through both sides to close the gap. Fasten off.

To close up the top of the cap

attach a darning needle to the **long starting tail** and weave in and out of the stitches along the very edge at the top as pictured. Then pull it tightly - because there are so many rows it will not close up entirely so you will want to take the tail (still on the needle) and sew the gap closed from back to front.

You can use the remainder of the tail to sew the cap onto your dolls head. Sew through a st on every row (between the ridges) working in and out of the head all the way around at the level of the bangs/fringe. This will allow the 'hair' at the bottom to flow out freely from the head and look more natural.

TOO BIG? TOO SMALL? SEE PAGE 25

HRH The Queen Hair

This hair cap is worked in **rows** **from the top down**.

Row 1: Leaving a long starting tail, ch25, hdc into the second chain from the hook, hdc into each of the next 10 chains, work 3hdc into each of the next 2 chains, hdc into each of the remaining 11 chains, turn (28sts)

Row 2: Ch1 (not a st from now on), hdc into each of the first 11sts, work 2hdc into each of the next 2sts, hdc into each of the next 2sts, work 2hdc into each of the next 2sts, hdc into each of the remaining 11sts, turn (32sts)

Row 3: Ch1, hdc into each of the first 11sts, work 2hdc into each of the next 2sts, hdc into each of the next 6sts, work 2hdc into each of the next 2sts, hdc into each of the remaining 11sts, turn (36sts)

Row 4: Ch1, hdc into each of the first 12sts, work 2hdc into each of the next 2sts, hdc into each of the next 8sts, work 2hdc into each of the next 2sts, hdc into each of the remaining 12sts, turn (40sts)

Row 5: Ch1, hdc into each of the first 12sts, work 2hdc into each of the next 2sts, hdc into each of the next 12sts, work 2hdc into each of the next 2sts, hdc into each of the remaining 12sts, turn (44sts)

TOO BIG? TOO SMALL? SEE PAGE 25

Row 6: Ch1, hdc into each st across, turn (44sts)

Row 7: Ch1, hdc into each st across, turn (44sts)

Row 8: Ch1, hdc into each st across, turn (44sts)

Row 9: Ch1, hdc into each st across, turn (44sts)

Row 10: Ch1, hdc into each st across, turn (44sts)

Row 11: Ch1, hdc2tog x2, hdc into each of the next 36sts, hdc2tog x2, turn (40sts)

Row 12: Ch1, hdc2tog x2, hdc into each of the next 32sts, hdc2tog x2, turn (36sts)

Row 13: Ch1, sc2tog x2, sc into each of the next 28sts, sc2tog x2, turn (32sts)

Row 14: Ch1, sc2tog x2, sc into each of the next 10sts, sc2tog x2, sc into each of the next 10sts, sc2tog x2, turn (26sts)

Fasten off, leaving a long tail for sewing the cap onto the head.

Attach a darning needle to the long starting tail and sew the two edges at the top together to create the parting, as pictured (on a similar cap in purple) here.

To sew the cap onto the head…
Continue to use the finishing tail to sew the hair cap to head using a whip st – please see the video on the Weebee and Friends YouTube channel if you need help with this. I found it helpful to pin this particular cap into place to make sure that it sat in the correct place and didn't move as I sewed.

Fasten off and hide loose ends.

Front Hair Piece

I would recommend working with as small a hook as is comfortable for this particular part of the pattern so that the curls are nice and tight and don't end up looking too bulky.

TOO BIG? TOO SMALL? SEE PAGE 25

Leaving a long starting tail, ch33, check the length of the chain reaches comfortably from one side of the hair cap to the other from just above the ear to just above the opposite ear.

If it is too short, try chaining again with a bigger hook, if it's too big try with a smaller hook.

Alternatively, simply chain a length that fits that is a multiple of 2 and then chain one extra – bare in mind, if you do this that your end stitch counts will differ from the ones here.

Row 1: Sc into the second ch from the hook, sc into each remaining ch across, turn (32sts)

Row 2: Ch1 (not a st), work 3hdc into each st across, turn (96sts)

Row 3: Ch2 (not a st), work 3dc into each st across (288sts)

Fasten off and hide the finishing tail.

Straighten up the starting chain and sew the hair piece onto the head at the front – the piece will be twisting and turning but that's what it needs to do to create the curls but it must be sewn straight along the edge of the hair cap from just above one ear to the next as pictured. You can then manipulate the curls back in the centre to create her majesty's iconic curls.

Curls for the back – make 6

Rnd 1: Leaving a long starting tail, MR, ch1 (not a st from now on), work 6sc, join the last st to the first with a sl st (6sts)

Rnd 2: Ch1, work 3hdc into each st around, join as before (18sts)

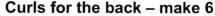
TOO BIG? TOO SMALL? SEE PAGE 25

Rnd 3: Ch2 (not a st), work 4dc into each st around, join (72sts)

Fasten off and hide the finishing tail.

Use the starting tail to sew the curl onto the head beneath the hair cap as pictured.

If you place one at either side and work towards the middle you can make sure that the curls cover the gap from ear to ear – you'll then know whether to make more or less curls to suit because your doll may differ to mine due to yarn brand etc.

TOO BIG? TOO SMALL? SEE PAGE 25

Most Versatile Cap

A Little About How This Cap Came About

I came across this photo online of a manufactured doll head prepared for the placement of hair strands and I began to wonder if I could create a pattern for a hair cap that would allow a crocheter to apply strands in the same kind of rows, to allow full head coverage.

This hair cap is worked in **rows from the top down**, a special technique is used in order to create rows of double loops on the top side of the cap on every other row. You can then add strands of yarn or crochet onto these loops to create 'hair'.

Row 1: Leaving a long starting tail, ch25, hdc into the **back bump (see special techniques on page 16)** of the second ch from the hook, hdc into the **back bump** of each of the next 10chs, work 3hdc into the **back bump** of each of the next 2chs, hdc into the **back bump** of each of the remaining 11chs, turn (28sts)

Row 2: In this row, you will be working on the wrong side of the hair cap (the underside), AND you will be working into the lowest loop at the front of the work for each st – this will create the double chain loops on the right side of

TOO BIG? TOO SMALL? SEE PAGE 25

the work, please see photos below for clarification. Ch1 (not a st from now on), hdc into each of the first 11sts, work 2hdc into each of the next 2sts, hdc into each of the next 2sts, work 2hdc into each of the next 2sts, hdc into each of the remaining 11sts, turn (32sts)

Regular loops – front and back NOT THESE

Lowest loop on front of work – creates double chain loops on the right side of the cap

Photo showing rows of double chain loops that you can crochet strands of hair onto

Row 3: Ch1, hdc into each of the first 11sts, work 2hdc into each of the next 2sts, hdc into each of the next 6sts, work 2hdc into each of the next 2sts, hdc into each of the remaining 11sts, turn (36sts)

Pause to sew the parting - Take a darning needle and attach it to the long starting chain. Then close up the parting by identifying the back loops on either side, as pictured below and then sewing through them - this will leave a loop on either side of the parting to add more hair to if necessary - see photo in orange.

Row 4: Again, work these stitches into the lower front loops (see photo's on previous page). Ch1, hdc into each of the first 12sts, work 2hdc into each of

TOO BIG? TOO SMALL? SEE PAGE 25

the next 2sts, hdc into each of the next 8sts, work 2hdc into each of the next 2sts, hdc into each of the remaining 12sts, turn (40sts)

Row 5: Ch1, hdc into each of the first 12sts, work 2hdc into each of the next 2sts, hdc into each of the next 12sts, work 2hdc into each of the next 2sts, hdc into each of the remaining 12sts, turn (44sts)

Row 6: Lower front loops! Ch1, hdc into each st across, turn (44sts)

Row 7: Ch1, hdc into each st across, turn (44sts)

Row 8: Lower front loops! Ch1, hdc into each st across, turn (44sts)

Row 9: Ch1, hdc2tog x2, hdc into each of the next 36sts, hdc2tog x2, turn (40sts)

Row 10: Lower front loops! Ch1, hdc into each st across, turn (40sts)

Row 11: Ch1, hdc2tog x2, hdc into each of the next 32sts, hdc2tog x2, turn (36sts)

Row 12: Lower front loops! Ch1, hdc into each st across, turn (36sts)

Row 13: Ch1, hdc2tog x2, hdc into each of the next 28sts, hdc2tog x2, turn (32sts)

Row 14: Lower front loops! Ch1, hdc into each st across, turn (32sts)

Row 15: Ch1, hdc2tog x2, hdc into each of the next 10sts, hdc2tog x2, hdc into each of the next 10sts, hdc2tog x2, turn (26sts)

Row 16: Ch1, hdc2tog x2, hdc into each of the next 7sts, hdc2tog x2, hdc into each of the next 7sts, hdc2tog x2, turn (20sts)

Fasten off, leaving a long tail for sewing the cap onto the head later.

TOO BIG? TOO SMALL? SEE PAGE 25

How to Make Different Types of Hair Strands

In the following paragraphs I explain how to create any length and type of hair strand. If you want the hair to be all the same length, you will need to decide your length on the bottom row and then ch more for each strand above. Feel free to experiment and have fun with the versatile hair cap – you can also use hdc or dc stitches to create thicker strands. Each of these examples shows a ch21 strand. Bear in mind that if you are working any type of curl that the strand will work up shorter than the amount you chain.

To Create Straight Hair Strands

Chain desired length of hair strand, sl st LOOSELY into the second ch from the hook, sl st LOOSELY into each remaining ch back towards the cap, sl st into the next st. You can work these strands in every st on the hair cap or sl st into the next st to create less strands and less weight depending on the coverage you require. Repeat this process until you reach the end of the row you are working on – you do not have to fasten off until you reach the end or unless you are changing colours.

To Create Loose Wavy Hair Strands

Chain desired length of hair strand, ^sc into the second ch from the hook, sc into each remaining ch back towards the cap, sl st into the next st. You can work these strands in every st on the hair cap or sl st into the next st to create less strands and less weight depending on the coverage you require. Repeat this process until you reach the end of the row you are working on – you do not have to fasten off until you reach the end or unless you are changing colours.

TOO BIG? TOO SMALL? SEE PAGE 25

^If you find that working one sc into each st doesn't give you enough of a curl, try working 2sc in every st or in every other st.

To Create Tendrils (straight at the top, curly at the bottom)

Chain desired length of hair strand, ^sc into the second ch from the hook, sc into half of the remaining chs back towards the cap, sl st into each remaining ch, sl st into the next st. You can work these strands in every st on the hair cap or sl st into the next st to create less strands and less weight depending on the coverage you require. Repeat this process until you reach the end of the row you are working on – you do not have to fasten off until you reach the end or unless you are changing colours.

^If you find that working one sc into each st doesn't give you enough of a curl, try working 2sc in every st or in every other st.

To Create Kinks in Your Hair Strands

Chain desired length of hair strand, sl st LOOSELY into the second ch from the hook, sl st LOOSELY into each remaining ch back towards the cap **ADDING** 2sc or 3sc into random chs to create more of a kink in that location, sl st into the next st on the cap. You can work these strands in every st or sl st into the next st to create less strands and less weight depending on the coverage you require. With kinks like these you do not have to repeat the same for each strand as it will look more natural the more random the kinks are. Repeat this process until you reach the end of the row you are working on – you do not have to fasten off until you reach the end or unless you are changing colours.

TOO BIG? TOO SMALL? SEE PAGE 25

The more sts you work into the ch the curlier the strand.

To Create Curly Hair Strands

Chain desired length of hair strand (baring in mind that curly hair works up a lot shorter), work 2sc (or 3sc) into the second ch from the hook, work 2sc (or 3sc) into each remaining ch back towards the cap, sl st into the next st. You can work these strands into every st or sl st into the next st to create less strands and less weight depending on the coverage you require. Repeat this process until you reach the end of the row you are working on – you do not have to fasten off until you reach the end or unless you are changing colours.

TOO BIG? TOO SMALL? SEE PAGE 25

Straight Bob Hair

How to start...

Begin by making the versatile hair cap on pages 70 - 72 in your chosen yarn colour

I would recommend using the same hook size that you used to make your doll to make thie hair cap, providing you are using the same brand and weight of yarn **BUT I would strongly recommend going up at least one whole hook size for the hair strands.** Bear in mind though that when you are working with curls instead, the smaller the hook size, the tighter the curls and vice versa so you may want to experiment ifyou're not happy with how your strands are working up.

Work with the hair onto the cap upside down, attach your yarn to the right hand side and start working your strands from the bottom layer upwards

I chose to work the bottom strands in every other st as pictured here.

I worked the next layer and the very top layer into every st as pictured here.

TOO BIG? TOO SMALL? SEE PAGE 25

In every other layer I chose to work into every other st so that the cap wouldn't be too heavy. To make the hair all one length I chained more the higher up the cap I worked.

For this cap here's what I did – I wanted to try to keep the hair all one length, so I decided to make the bottom layer the guide for the length of each layer.	
Bottom Layer	Attach yarn. *Ch5, sl st LOOSELY into the second ch from the hook, sl st LOOSELY into each of the remaining 3chs, sl st into the next st, sl st into the next st, repeat from * to end. Fasten off and hide loose ends.
Next Layer Up	Attach yarn. *Ch9, sl st LOOSELY into the second ch from the hook, sl st LOOSELY into each of the remaining 7chs, sl st into the next st, repeat from * to end. Fasten off and hide loose ends.
Next Layer Up	Attach yarn. *Ch11, sl st LOOSELY into the second ch from the hook, sl st LOOSELY into each of the remaining 9chs, sl st into the next st, sl st into the next st, repeat from * to end. Fasten off and hide loose ends.
Next Layer Up	Attach yarn. *Ch13, sl st LOOSELY into the second ch from the hook, sl st LOOSELY into each of the remaining 11chs, sl st into the next st, sl st into the next st, repeat from * to end. Fasten off and hide loose ends.
Next Layer Up	Attach yarn. *Ch15, sl st LOOSELY into the second ch from the hook, sl st LOOSELY into each of the remaining 13chs, sl st into the next st, sl st into the next st, repeat from * to end. Fasten off and hide loose ends.
Next Layer Up	Attach yarn. *Ch17, sl st LOOSELY into the second ch from the hook, sl st LOOSELY into each of the remaining 15chs, sl st into the next st, sl st into the next st, repeat from * to end. Fasten off and hide loose ends.
Top Layer	Attach yarn. *Ch19, sl st LOOSELY into the second ch from the hook, sl st LOOSELY into each of the remaining 17chs, sl st into the next st, repeat from * to end. Fasten off and hide loose ends.

TOO BIG? TOO SMALL? SEE PAGE 25

It might not be necessary for every cap you make but if like me, you decide that the **parting needs covering you can make a separate hair piece and sew it on to cover the parting - you can also make shorter strands to place at the front in this way to make bangs/a fringe.**

How to make a hair piece to cover the parting and/or add a fringe/bangs!

Ch11 for the parting (or ch less to make a fringe (bangs) piece), *ch desired length for hair strand (I chained 23), sl st (or sc for curls) into the second ch from the hook. Sl st (or sc for curls) into each ch until you reach the original set of original chs (I worked a sl st into 22chs and in my case I had chained 11 to cover the parting so stopped there), sl st into the next ch, repeat from * until you have as many strands as you originally chained in total, fasten off leaving a long tail.

Sew into place on the cap, either to one side to cover the parting or at the front to make bangs.

TOO BIG? TOO SMALL? SEE PAGE 25

Cornrow Braids

Start by making the versatile hair cap on pages 70 -72 using the **same skin tone yarn** that you used to make the doll.

Begin by attaching your yarn for the hair strands to the cap at the front of cap as pictured.

Then work a LOOSE sl st into each st until you reach the back of the cap, then stop and TURN (so the centre of the row – see arrow)

Sl st LOOSELY along the underside of the stitches into the lowest skin tone yarn colour as pictured above until you reach the front of the cap again. TURN.

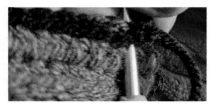

Ch1, and work a tw sc (see special stitches on page 14) into the underside of the first set of sl sts you worked, over and around the ridge made by the previous two rows of sl sts (see photo).

TOO BIG? TOO SMALL? SEE PAGE 25

When you reach the last st at the back, ch any length you desire for the braid, (I chained 31) then turn and work a sl st into the second ch from the hook and sl st into each of the remaining chs back to the cap. Fasten off and hide loose ends.

Repeat these steps for the opposite side of the row you worked on first and then all the way down to the very bottom of the cap.

You can even repeat these steps onto the very edge of the cap.

Once all of your cornrows and braids have been made, reattach your yarn to the right hand side of the cap at the front as pictured and work tw sc evenly from one side to the other.

Fasten off leaving a good long tail.

Use the tail to sew the cap onto your doll's head. Making sure along the front to make some extra long stitches between the rows, this makes it look more like real hair.

TOO BIG? TOO SMALL? SEE PAGE 25

To make a pony tail, take a length of yarn in the same colour as the hair and gather up the braids at the back as pictured, wrap the length of yarn around them, tie up and secure into place.

You can thicken up the ponytail by making a length of strands - simply chain the same length you chained for the braid at the back of the cap. To add a pop of colour simply work 2 strands of yarn together!

Then simply sew these strands in to place where the ponytail meets the cap as pictured.

TOO BIG? TOO SMALL? SEE PAGE 25

Twisted Hair Strands

Bottom Layer

Start by making the versatile hair cap on pages 70-72 using your chosen yarn colour and then with the cap held the **right way up** attach yarn to the right hand side of the hair cap to the first set of unworked double chain loops at the bottom- I used 2 strands held together (black and brown) but feel free to experiment with different amounts of strands and different colours.

Ch1 and make the loop twice as long as you'd like your hair length to be (I used the length of an A4 piece of paper folded in half as a guide for mine but you could use a book or a piece of paper/card cut to length), then twist the loop (or loops if using two yarns together) with your hook around 16-30 times depending on the length of your loops - for the short strands on my doll. I rotated mine 16 times, for longer strands you will need to twist more, then sl st into the same st on the hair cap - the long twisted chain should automatically twist together into shape when you work the sl st. Sl st into each of the next 2sts, then repeat from * to * just as you did to create the first strand. When you reach the opposite end,

TOO BIG? TOO SMALL? SEE PAGE 25

Fasten off.

Tip: This is the same method many people use to add a fringe to their crocheted blankets so if you need help with this, simply head to your search engine or onto social media and search for 'twisted crochet fringe' to find further information and videos on how to work these.

The Next Three Layers Up
Follow instructions for bottom layer.

Top Two Layers
In these two layers you will be repeating the strands as before but in every st across, rather than every other st. So, with the cap held right side up, attach yarn(s) to the right hand side of the hair cap to the first set of unworked double chain loops as before.

Ch1 and make the desired length of loop then twist the loop as before, then sl st into the same st on the hair. Sl st into the next st*, then repeat from * to * . When you reach the opposite end, fasten off.

I didn't add any extra strands to the loops on the parting because I didn't feel it needed them but if you do, feel free to add extra strands there - using the loops show on the orange pic on page 71.

Finally hide any loose ends before sewing cap onto the head.

TOO BIG? TOO SMALL? SEE PAGE 25

Doll Hair Wefts

To add hair wefts to the cap, you will need to purchase at least three 100cm widths of 15-20cm long doll hair wefts. I used three different shades of pink to create this look here.

Start by making a versatile hair cap in either skin tone yarn or in a similar colour to the wefts you are going to sew on, then sew the cap into place on the dolls head.

I did this afterwards and regretted not doing it first, it will be a lot easier to do beforehand.

Then working from the bottom set of double chain loops up, pin the first weft into place and cut to the correct width, then you will simply take a small needle and some thread in a similar colour and sew the weft into place as pictured.

TOO BIG? TOO SMALL? SEE PAGE 25

Continue to work upwards adding a weft to each set of double chain loops.

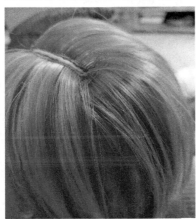

When you reach the top you can sew a couple of shorter wefts to the cap itself on either side as pictured to create a parting and cover the space on top.

Secure and hide any loose threads.

TOO BIG? TOO SMALL? SEE PAGE 25

Long Straight Hair

Start by making the versatile hair cap using your chosen yarn colour and then continue as follows...

Lowest Set of Loops

With the cap held upside down attach yarn to the lowest set of loops on the right hand side. Ch17, sl st LOOSELY into the second ch from the hook, sl st into each of the remaining 15chs back up to the cap. Sl st into the same st on the cap, sl st into each of the next 3sts on the cap. Repeat from * to end. Make sure to end with a strand in the second to last or last set of loops, whether you have to sl st st into the loops or not - this ensures a neat look.

The Next Two Layers Up

Follow instructions for the lowest set of loops above but **chain 19** for the first layer up and then **chain 21** for the next layer up.

Top Two Layers

In these two layers you will be repeating the strands as before but in every other st across, rather than every third st. So, with the cap held wrong side up, attach yarn tothe right hand side of the hair cap to the first set of unworked double chain loops as before.

TOO BIG? TOO SMALL? SEE PAGE 25

First Layer: Ch23, sl st LOOSELY into the second ch from the hook, sl st into each of the remaining 21chs back up to the cap. Sl st into the same st on the cap, sl st into each of the next 2sts on the cap. Repeat from * to end. Making sure again to end with a strand in the second to last or last set of loops, whether you have to sl st st into the loops or not - this ensures a neat look.

Next Layer: As in layer above but chain 25 rather than 23.

Parting

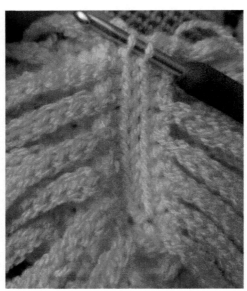

Working from the front of the cap to the back,
insert your hook through both loops on either side as pictured. *Ch27, sl st LOOSELY into the second ch from the hook, sl st LOOSELY into each of the remaining 25chs across, sl st into the next st, repeat from * across. Fasten off and hide loose ends.

To sew the cap onto the head...

Continue to use the finishing tail to sew the hair cap to head using a whip st – please visit the Weebee and Friends YouTube channel for a video showing how to do this if you need help. Fasten off and hide loose ends.

TOO BIG? TOO SMALL? SEE PAGE 25

Ponytails, Pigtails, Plaits, Buns and Bunches...

Ponytail

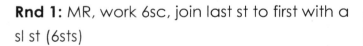

(or for chunky pigtails, simply make 2 and sew one to either side of the head)

Rnd 1: MR, work 6sc, join last st to first with a sl st (6sts)

Rnd 2: *Ch21, work ^^2sc into second ch from hook, continue to work 2sc in each of the next 9chs, sc in each remaining ch back towards the circle, sl st back into same st and repeat from *once more into the st before working a sl st into the next st.

Repeat from * into every st around, sl st into first st again after working the last tendril (12 tendrils)

^^if you find that working 2sc is not curly enough, you can try working 3sc instead. Alternatively you can go down a hook size or two to create tighter stitches and therefore a better curl.

Fasten off leaving a long tail.

Weave the tail in and out around the first round of stitches (6sts) and pull tight to gather it together, then insert your needle through the point created in the centre of the circle before sewing the tendrils onto the side of the hair cap, working through stitches on the cap and the head for a secure fastening – there is a video on the Weebee and Friends YouTube shows how I sew my curls on.

Pigtails

*Ch13, work 2hdc in second ch from hook and in each ch to end, repeat from * twice more. Fasten off leaving a long tail.

Then simply sew one set of hair curls on to each side of the head, low down if you want the doll to wear a hat.

Plaits & Braids

These plaits can be used to make ponytail plaits, pigtail plaits, or even wrapped around the doll's head.

1. Start by chaining 3.

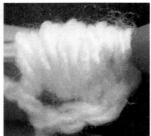

2. Work PS (see special stitches on page 14) in third ch from hook.

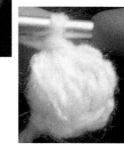

3. Ch2 and turn.

4. *Work a PS into the ch2 space before the previous PS

5. Ch2 and turn…

Repeat from * until the braid is as long as you need it to be. Then fasten off leaving a long tail and sew into place on doll's head. Hide starting tail and fastening off tail when sewn into place.

You can make them with 3dc puff stitches as per this picture tutorial or experiment with 4+dc puff stitches to create thicker plaits or use two colours of yarn to create two tone plaits.

Feel free to try different yarn weights too and work different lengths, just have fun with them!

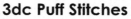

4dc Puff Stitches

3dc Puff Stitches

3dc Puff Stitches with 2 yarns held together

3dc Puff Stitches

Hair Bun

This bun is worked in joined rounds, at the end of each round join the last st to the top of the first with a sl st.

Rnd 1: MR, ch1 (not a st from now on) and work 11hdc, join (as above) (11sts)

Rnd 2: Ch1, work 2hdc in the **back loop only** of each st around, join (22sts)

Rnd 3: Ch1, hdc in **back loop only** of the first st, work 2hdc in the **back loop only** of the next st, *hdc in the **back loop only** of next st, work 2hdc in the **back loop only** of the next st, repeat from * around, join (33sts)

Rnd 4: Ch1, hdc in the **back loop only** of the first two sts, 2hdc in the **back loop only** of the next st, *hdc in the **back loop only** of the next two sts, 2hdc in the **back loop only** of the next st, repeat from * around, join (44sts)

Rnds 5 & 6^^: Ch1, hdc in the **back loop only** of each st around (forms a small cup shape) (44sts)

^^ Feel free to work more rounds of 44sts for a taller bun.

Fasten off and leave a long tail for sewing the bun to the hair cap – I sew my cap on first and then position the bun and sew it into place - stuff the bun lightly, position your bun as desired and then sew through the two loops on the stitches on the outer edge of the bun to stitches on the hair cap.

Hair Bunches

Here's how to make a hair bunch – make as many as you like and feel free to experiment with the length of the chains and the amount of bunches you make to suit...

MR, *ch5, sl st back into the MR, repeat from * 7 more times, until you have 8 loops, close the MR and fasten off leaving a long tail. Use tail to sew the bunch(es) into desired position on the head working through both the stitches on the cap and the doll's for a secure fastening.

Space Bun

Here's how to make a messy little space bun – make as many as you like and feel free to experiment with the length of the strands.

Rnd 1: MR, ch1 (not a st from now on), work 6sc, join the last st to the first with a sl st (6sts)

Rnd 2: Ch1, work 2sc into each st around, join as before (12sts)

Strands: *Ch17, sl st into the second ch from the hook, continue to sl st LOOSELY into each of the remaining 15chs, sl st into the same st in rnd 2, sl st into the next st, repeat from * around until you have 12 strands of 'hair'. Then fasten off leaving a long tail.

Begin by hiding the starting tail, then pin the circle you made (rnds 1 & 2) into the desired location on the doll's head, end by using the fastening off tail to sew the circle into place, working through the stitches between the strands, the stitches on the hair cap and the stitched on the doll's head where possible.

To turn the pigtails into buns, simply tie the strands together, tying one or two strands together opposite one another until you're happy with how they look.

Experimenting with Different Yarns...

There have been two occasions in the past where members of the Facebook group absolutely adored the hair caps on two of my dolls and requested patterns for them from me when all I had done was simply experiment with yarn!

Variegated Yarns

Variegated yarn is multi-coloured yarn that is dyed in sections. The coloured sections may appear in a random order or in a set pattern.

Either way, the streaks of different colours in variegated yarn can create interesting effects in your hair caps.

A few years ago whilst on holiday I visited a store in the UK and found a really pretty variegated yarn.

I often buy a skein of yarn here and there thinking that they might come in useful for one of my patterns one day.

I decided to try this particular one on a hair cap for my new doll and to my surprise it worked up beautifully.

It pooled in just the right places, creating soft pink vertical stripes and horizontal rounds of brown and cream.

Believe it or not the hair cap I made is simply the basic cap you'll find within this book on page 26 and the pigtails are the ones included with the Buttercup hair in this book which you will find on page 59.

I told people which yarn I'd used but it wasn't a well known brand. Only one person managed to get hold of it and it worked up completely differently for them. This was because you would have to have the exact same dye lot, the exact same personal gauge/tension and have started in exactly the same place as me on the skein to get the same or at least a very similar effect.

Fun Fur Yarns

Also known as eyelash yarn, these furry yarns are perfect for crocheting toys and fluffy edgings as well as fun garments for little ones. With no stitch definition, the yarn creates a furry fabric that is easy to crochet, even for beginners.

I often get asked for a pattern for this particular cap which I made back in 2016, but it was so straight forward that again there's really no need for a written pattern.

I simply held two strands of yarn together, one was Stylecraft Eskimo DK in Old Gold and the other was Stylecraft Special DK in Mocha (similar colours). I used a hook that felt comfortable and made the basic hair cap (see page 26), stopping the increases when the cap fit and working straight rounds of dc from there. I'm sure that I added or missed a stitch here or there as it's not easy to see the stitches particularly but as you can see it's so thick that you can't tell. I also preferred the look of the 'wrong' side and sewed it that way around onto the head.

What to consider...

To make the most of your yarn selection, consider the following:

- Before starting a project, research what type of fiber is best suited for your desired outcome.

- Experiment with different yarn blends to achieve specific qualities or effects.

- Consider the care instructions for your chosen fiber to ensure longevity of your finished piece.

By taking these factors into account while exploring the diverse world of yarn fibres, you'll be well-equipped to create beautiful and functional pieces that perfectly suit your creative vision.

Creating your own Hair Cap Designs!

So you have a request or an idea for a cap that there seems to be no suitable Weebee pattern for at the moment. It's so frustrating isn't it! So here are a few hints and tips to get you on your way to coming up with what you need and failing these don't forget that you can always drop me a line on Facebook or Ravelry to see if I can help!

Try Different Stitch Combinations

To begin with I would highly recommend getting hold of a crochet stitches book so that you can experiment with combinations of different stitches. It's simply a case of working those stitch combinations in the round to 55-66sts and then working straight from there to create your own unique hair cap! There are lots of these books available so take a look and see which one suits you best. If you don't have the funds for a book at the moment, you can find a lot of different stitches online. Simply type 'interesting crochet stitch' or something like 'textured crochet stitch' into a search engine and you should get lots of results. You could do the same searches on YouTube for video tutorial results or Pinterest so that you could pin them and keep them safe for future use.

How About A Hat?

Try searching for 'crochet hat' online and you'll find so many beautiful ones, now imagine them in a colour suitable for hair, with a little parting at the front and either buns or pigtails on the side and what do you have? A fabulous hair cap design for your doll!

Research Other Ideas

There are so many ideas for hair for your dolls freely available online if you know where to look. Head to your search engine or YouTube and type in 'amigurumi doll hair' and you'll get so many interesting ideas looking through the search results!

As you become more experienced, you can experiment with different yarn techniques and stitches.

Consider using a bobble stitch, puff stitch, popcorn stitch, or a post stitch to create intricate patterns and textures.

You'll also want to learn how to care for your projects and the different types of yarn so that your pieces stay looking like new.

Once you feel comfortable with the basics, the possibilities are endless!

As you continue to hone your skills, don't be afraid to try new things and take risks when you start crocheting.

About the Author

Laura Tegg is an established crochet pattern designer. What began as a childhood hobby has become her full-time job, with thousands of crocheters turning to her patterns daily for their well-written, user-friendly instructions and adorable results.

She lives and continues to design and crochet non-stop in Cumbria in the UK alongside her husband Andrew their daughter and their French Bulldog, Bree.

Her popular standard size Weebee Doll pattern was first published in 2016 and you can find that pattern and hundreds of others (over 40 of them for free) at ravelry.com.

In 2023 Laura self published her first physical book 'Hooked on Weebee' which can be found on amazon,com

I would like to thank every single member of the Weebee Appreciation Society on Facebook for supporting me over the last 7 years. Your support and input has been absolutely invaluable.

I would also be nowhere without my wonderful Facebook modmin team and pattern testers - Alicia, Bianca, Christie, Liz and Shannon. Not only have you helped to ensure that my patterns are error free, understandable and user friendly but you have also become very dear friends to me over the last few years. I would truly be lost without you!

And last but in no means least I would like to thank my fabulous family for all of their enthusiasm, support and encouragement.

Also Available

Within the **Hooked on Weebee** book you will find everything you need to crochet your very own adorable standard size Weebee doll and a set of removable clothes for them to wear!

Weebee is a no sew doll, made all in one from the feet up - even the arms are crocheted on! With straightforward, easy to follow, step by step instructions even the less experienced crocheter should find the patterns within easy to follow.

Those of you familiar with Weebee, might be wondering what's new. Well, this new version of the doll includes a brand new neck support! There are also three new options for the versatile hair cap - which has also been improved, as well as over 30 items of clothing and accessories never before published!

Mix and match the hair caps and clothing to create the perfect doll for you or a mini me for someone you love!

This 59 page book includes the standard size Weebee doll pattern with a new and improved neck support and over 30 items of clothing and accessories.

What's included:
- Weebee Doll Pattern with new neck support!
- New & Improved Versatile Hair Cap

Clothing:
- Sleeveless Top
- T-shirt
- Long Sleeved Tee/Sweater
- Sleeveless Dress
- Dress with Short Sleeves
- Dress with Long Sleeves
- Playsuit
- Jumpsuit
- Jacket/Cardigan
- Hoodie
- Skirt
- Trousers
- Shorts/Underwear
- Shoes
- Sneakers
- Boots
- Sandals
- Mittens/Gloves
- Scarf
- Beanie Hat
- Sun Visor
- Baseball Cap
- Headband
- Brimmed Hat
- Open Top Summer Hat
- Shoulder Bag
- Backpack

Plus much more!

From Amazon!*

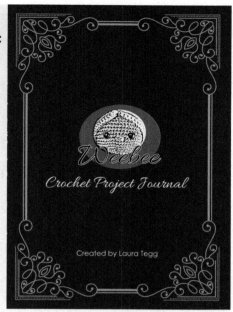

This **185-page, A5-size journal has been designed for fans of the Weebee doll crochet patterns,** which are all available from www.ravelry.com. Over 40 of them for free, including dolls and removable outfits for each one!

This journal is not only useful for recording your projects but is also packed full of helpful information such as where to find all of the patterns, a quick guide to each of the Weebee Dolls including their size and which size safety eyes to use as well as a visual guide to the hair caps currently available for all of the dolls!

Please note that this journal does not contains any crochet patterns, it is a journal/logbook with helpful guides.

Lots of useful information!

Numbered Pages & Index

30 Project Pages!

Hair Cap Guide

Weebee Doll Pattern Checklist

Yarn Stash Pages

Set Your Goals

*unfortunately journal is not available in all territories

Where to find out more...

Find the patterns here:

Online: www.weebeedolls.com

Ravelry: www.ravelry.com/designers/laura-tegg

Etsy: www.etsy.com/shop/WeebeeDolls

Youtube: Weebee and Friends

Follow the Weebee Dolls here:

Facebook: Weebee Appreciation Society

Tiktok: @weebeedolls

Instagram: @lollyscc

Support Laura here:

Patreon: www.patreon.com/weebeedolls

Ko-fi: www,ko-fi.com/weebeedolls

Weebee

Please share your Weebee projects with us in the Weebee Appreciation Society Facebook Group and don't forget to add your project to Ravelry!

I really hope that you enjoy completing the items within this book and look forward to seeing them online!

Laura xx

#weebeedoll
#weebeedollhaircap
#weebeeappreciationsociety
#laurategg
#crochetdollpattern
#amigurumi

Printed in Great Britain
by Amazon